THE CANADIAN ROCKIES

BRUCE OBEE

Whitecap Books

Vancouver / Toronto

The information in this book is true and complete to the best of our
knowledge. All recommendations are made without guarantee on the part
of the author or Whitecap Books Ltd. The author and publisher disclaim
any liability in connection with the use of this information. For additional
information please contact Whitecap Books Ltd., 1086 West Third Street,
North Vancouver, B.C., V7P 3J6.

Edited by Elaine Jones
Cover design by Warren Clark
Interior design by Margaret Ng
Cover photograph by Darwin Wiggett / First Light
Typeset by CompuType

Printed and bound in Canada by D.W. Friesen and Sons Ltd.,
Altona, Manitoba

Canadian Cataloguing in Publication Data

Obee, Bruce, 1951-
  The Canadian Rockies

  ISBN 1-55110-163-7
  1. Rocky Mountains, Canadian (B.C. and Alta.)—Pictorial works. I. Title.
FC219.O23 1994   971.1′0022′2   C94-910021 8
F1090.O23 1994

CONTENTS

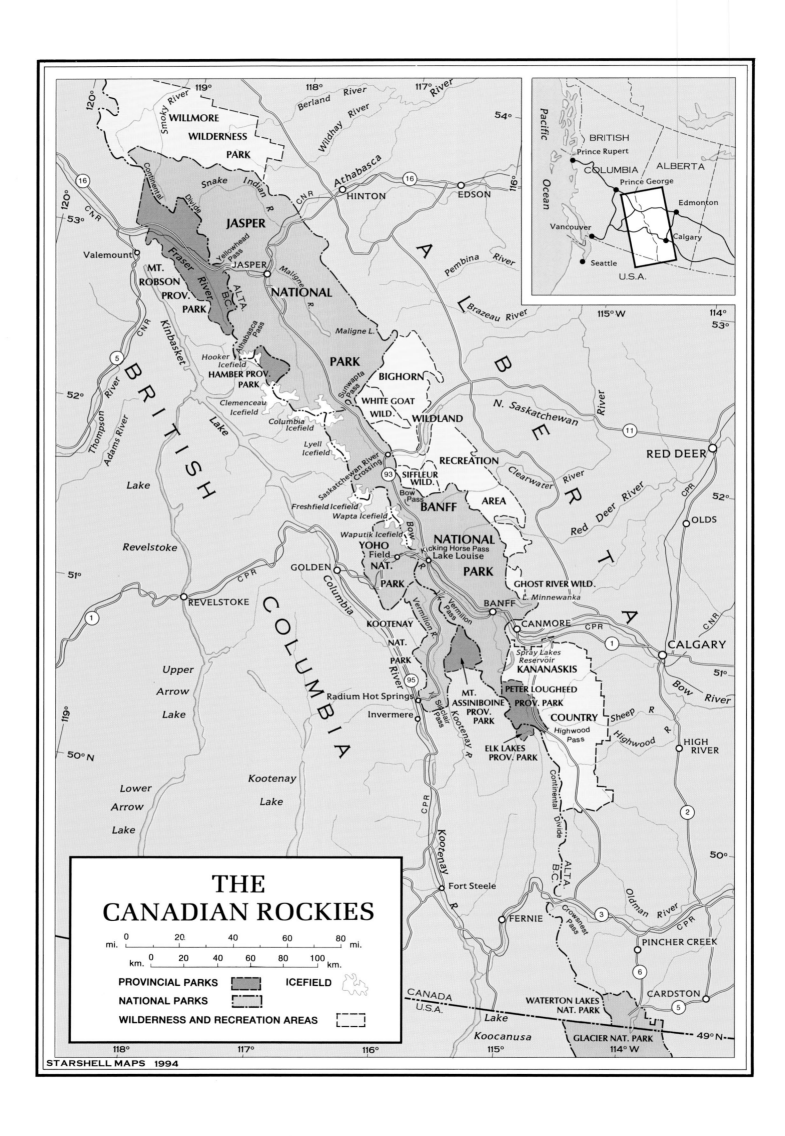

THE
CANADIAN ROCKIES

mi. 0   20   40   60   80 mi.

km. 0 20 40 60 80 100 km.

PROVINCIAL PARKS	ICEFIELD
NATIONAL PARKS	
WILDERNESS AND RECREATION AREAS	

STARSHELL MAPS 1994

Introduction

"If we can't export the scenery, we'll import the tourists."

William Cornelius Van Horne
1843-1915
Vice-president, Canadian Pacific Railway

There wasn't much going on in the Canadian Rockies before the railroad came through. The Ice Age had been over for ten thousand years: the glaciers, for the most part, had done their work. The Stoney Indians, like the grizzlies, were wandering at will when fur traders from the east crossed the Continental Divide.

This was a land unembellished by human endeavours. A place from which the rivers flowed unhindered and the mountains lay silent through the seasons. Only the animals—the predators and prey, the raptors and songbirds—were restless.

The Rockies changed forever with the coming of the railroad. As the last spike was driven on the Canadian Pacific Railway, Canada's first national park was designated at Banff, Alberta. These two events, in November, 1885, were more than mere coincidence: burdened by a heavy construction debt, the CPR was the most ardent supporter of preserving the scenery along the Rocky Mountain route. People with the means—globe-trotting Europeans, Americans, eastern Canadians—would gladly pay to see Canada's "fifty Switzerlands in one."

Trainloads of travellers were ensconced in elegant "chateaus" and "chalets," invariably overlooking the Rockies' most stunning rivers and lakes. They admired the scenery over cocktails in the courtyards, planning their guided forays into the unexplored hinterland. There were unconquered peaks and undiscovered waterfalls, valleys, and icefields. These magnificent mountains—a troublesome obstacle to fur brigades and railroad builders—had almost instantly become the nation's tourist mecca.

A century later, the Rocky Mountains still hold their prominence as Canada's premier vacationland: their monetary worth to an ever-growing tourism industry is undisputed. But more universally acknowledged, a century later, is their intrinsic value as one of the world's last vestiges of true mountain wilderness.

In 1985, during the centennial year of Banff National Park's inception, the United Nations Educational, Scientific, and Cultural Organization declared Banff and its neighbouring national parks—Kootenay, Yoho, and Jasper—a World Heritage Site. UNESCO's recognition of the Rocky Mountains' global significance ranks them with the Grand Canyon, the Egyptian Pyramids, the Galapagos Islands, and other great wonders of the world.

Five years later British Columbia's Mount Assiniboine, Hamber, and Mount Robson provincial parks joined the national parklands under UNESCO's protection. These Rocky Mountain parks, with other reserves along the B.C.-Alberta border, form a contiguous protected area of some thirty thousand square kilometres.

The Rockies are by no means North America's highest or oldest mountains, but their geographic influence reaches across the continent. For three thousand kilometres, from Santa Fe, New Mexico, to the Yukon's southern border, these mountains split North America into east and west. This Great Continental Divide is the birthplace of our mightiest rivers. In Canada, the Fraser and Columbia rivers run convoluted courses to the Pacific, six hundred kilometres west of the Rockies; the Saskatchewan River flows across the Prairies, through Lake Winnipeg into the Atlantic at Hudson Bay, sixteen hundred kilometres to the east; the Athabasca swells the waters of the Mackenzie River and pours into the Arctic Ocean, twenty-one hundred kilometres to the north. Though locked in the continental interior, the Rocky Mountains are united with all of North America's oceans by these rivers.

The glaciers that form their headwaters today are remnants of massive ice sheets that once straddled the Continental Divide. Creeping imperceptibly, these ponderous rivers of ice scraped and scoured for two million years, sculpting the distinctive landscapes that characterize the Rocky Mountains: wide U-shaped valleys, moraines, cirques, Matterhorn peaks, and sharp-crested ridges.

The trenches and troughs left in the wake of the glaciers are filled by meltwater that trickles down from the snow line. Rivulets merge as they tumble down the mountains to replenish the creeks and tarns. Growing as they travel, the streams thunder through canyons and plunge over sheer rock walls, continuing the work of the glaciers: scraping, scouring, sculpting.

They deliver all shades of emerald, azure, and turquoise to the high-elevation lakes, and reflections of the snowfields and peaks in the waters of Peyto, Maligne, Moraine, and other mountain lakes are especially vivid.

The big lakes are catchment basins for the headwaters of major rivers. Main streams like the Kootenay, Bow, Kicking Horse, Mistaya, North Saskatchewan, and Athabasca rivers are the natural highways of the Rockies. Grizzlies and black bears, deer, moose, and elk follow the river corridors through their seasonal migrations. Sure-footed mountain goats and bighorn sheep cling to craggy slopes above the rivers. Cougars, bobcats, lynx, wolves, and coyotes wander wherever there is prey. Some animals—marmots, pikas, ptarmigan—never leave the alpine, sharing the meadows with the wind and wildflowers.

Like the wildlife, the people of these mountains have traditionally travelled the waterways. They were pathways for nomadic native Indians, overland routes for fur traders. Eventually they became transportation corridors for the railways that brought the world to the heart of the Canadian Rockies.

By 1883 the tracks of the Canadian Pacific Railway were laid across the Prairies and up the Bow River to the doorstep of downtown Banff. They followed the river along the Alberta side of the Continental Divide to Lake Louise, then moved west over Kicking Horse Pass into British Columbia.

Sold by the railway's international campaign, throngs of tourists were lured to the Rockies and lodged in the CPR's swank hotels at Banff and Lake Louise. Many were content to sip tea on the terraces and marvel at the scenery. Others, hungry for a taste of genuine wilderness, hired horses and outfitters to take them into the outback. The more intrepid, afflicted by the "because-it's-there" syndrome, paid European guides, some of them imported by the railway, to lead them up unchallenged summits. In 1913 an Austrian guide, hired by the Alpine Club of Canada, led a Canadian and an American on the first successful ascent of Mount Robson's 3,954-metre peak, the highest in the Canadian Rockies.

That same year the Grand Trunk Pacific Railway came up the Athabasca River, through Jasper and over the divide at Yellowhead Pass, the route taken later by the Canadian Northern Railway. By 1922 Jasper, like the towns on the CPR line to the south, had its own hotel.

As Jasper Park Lodge hosted its first guests, new highways were penetrating the Rockies, following the rivers and railways through the towns and passes. Automobile touring became—and remains—the primary pastime of Rocky Mountain travellers. Over the years these mountain roads became known as the most scenic motorways in North America, some would say the world.

The highways, the tourist amenities, and the hiking trails that were built after the railroad came through changed the Rockies forever. But the essence of these mountains—the valleys and streams, the azure lakes and icefields, the peaks and alpine meadows, the wildlife and outback challenges—have changed little since the railway's arrival. The visionaries who protected the Canadian Rockies a century ago have left a legacy to share with the world for centuries to come.

Opposite: *The 3,618-metre peak of Mount Assiniboine is among the summits seen to the west of Kananaskis Country. The striking mountain, "the Matterhorn of the Canadian Rockies," is the centrepiece of the 391-square-kilometre provincial park established in 1922 and declared a UNESCO World Heritage Site in 1990.*

Banff
National Park

Banff is the birthplace of Canada's national parks. Since its tenuous beginnings as a nineteenth-century railway camp, Banff has grown to become the nation's prime tourist destination. It was here, in 1883, that railway workers on Sulphur Mountain stumbled upon Cave and Basin Hot Springs. Mindful of the popularity of European spas, in 1885 the federal government protected its newfound springs within a twenty-six-square-kilometre park reserve.

Two years later Rocky Mountains Park, 676 square kilometres of wild rivers, waterfalls, and unconquered peaks, was enticing well-to-do mountaineers and scenery seekers to its undiscovered environs. Comfortable in the coaches of the country's new transcontinental railway, American and European adventurers were delivered to the heart of the Canadian Rockies.

By 1888 the Banff Springs Hotel, built by the Canadian Pacific Railway, was greeting its first guests. Sporting the latest in outdoor attire, they planned their outings over tea and cocktails on the terrace above the Bow River. Their view was one of rugged beauty: pristine yet harsh, seductive yet forbidding. European mountain guides were hired to return the guests intact.

The old hotel, like the town around it, has grown in stature and grace, but the view is much the same: the glacier-green waters of the Bow River wander between the wooded slopes of Mount Rundle and Tunnel Mountain and disappear into the distant Fairholme Range. Amid the conifers today, the hotel's twenty-seven-hole golf course is an expansive manicured lawn. Across the river, beneath the meadows of Mount Norquay,

downtown Banff is abuzz with shoppers, sightseers, cyclists, and tour buses. Though only seven thousand people live here, three million come each year to admire its enviable setting.

Banff National Park was enlarged in 1930 to its current 6,640 square kilometres. Today, from its southern boundary west of Calgary, Alberta, to its border with Jasper National Park, it stretches more than two hundred kilometres along the eastern side of the Continental Divide. It is an immense mountain outback of turquoise lakes and glaciers, forests and alpine meadows, caves and hoodoos, wild rivers, plunging canyons, and steaming mineral pools.

The railway has faded from the limelight; paved highways carry a new generation of adventurers to viewpoints and trailheads throughout the park. More than thirteen hundred kilometres of trails penetrate the park: while some hikers are satisfied to stretch their legs a few hundred metres from their cars, others prefer to strap on a backpack and share the backwoods with grizzlies, eagles, and elk. With more than two dozen peaks over three thousand metres, the park beckons dauntless mountaineers and rock climbers searching for new challenges.

Although Banff is known worldwide for its downhill and cross-country skiing, the park and townsite virtually shut down each winter during its first three decades of existence. As small ski lodges were developed in the 1930s at nearby Sunshine Creek, and farther north at Lake Louise, Banff gradually became a year-round vacation centre. Today Banff retains its undisputed status as the centrepiece of Canada's Rocky Mountain parks.

Opposite: *The 2,998-metre peak of Cascade Mountain dominates the view of Banff Avenue, the main street in downtown Banff. Originally a railway camp known as Siding 29, Banff has become a community of seven thousand. About three million visitors enjoy this view each year.*

Above: Golfers at Banff Springs Hotel's twenty-seven-hole course enjoy views of Mount Rundle, Tunnel Mountain, and the Fairholme Range as they pursue their sport along the bank of the Bow River. Hikers on trails near the golf course enjoy the same views.

Opposite: Mount Rundle, at 2,949 metres, rises above Vermilion Lakes west of Banff. This mountain's so-called ''dip slope'' is characteristic of many in the Rocky's Front Ranges. Here the northeast face drops abruptly, while the southwest side has a more moderate slope.

Banff Springs Hotel

"If we can't export the scenery, we'll import the tourists," declared William Cornelius Van Horne, vice-president and general manager of the Canadian Pacific Railway. Faced with a huge debt from railway construction, it was the brain-child of Van Horne to build a chain of castlelike hotels at the most scenic points along the route. They would be filled with weary, and wealthy, train passengers.

Believing big is better, the CPR completed the largest hotel in the world in 1888. More than fifteen hundred guests registered at the Banff Springs during its first season. With automobiles banned from Banff National Park in the early years, the CPR had a virtual monopoly on transportation in and out of town. By the second season the Banff Springs hosted five thousand guests: the future of the tiny mountain community as a destination for international travellers was secured.

Located near the confluence of the Spray and Bow rivers, the hotel has undergone a number of renovations and expansions. The view from the hotel's terrace—the Bow River winding between Tunnel Mountain and Mount Rundle with the Fairholme Range in the distance—was very nearly enjoyed solely by the kitchen staff. When Van Horne examined the plans during construction, he found the building oriented backwards, with the terrace facing the woods.

Opposite: *Banff Springs Hotel overlooking the Bow River.*

Overleaf: *Citadel Pass, on the border between Banff National and Mount Assiniboine Provincial parks, lies about twenty-two kilometres southwest of Banff townsite. Hikers often tramp through the 2,608-metre pass from Banff's Sunshine Meadows on a three-day trek to Mount Assiniboine, the "Matterhorn" of the Canadian Rockies.*

Hot Springs

In 1883 railway workers stumbled upon Cave and Basin Hot Springs on Sulphur Mountain near Banff. A warm and comforting find in the midst of the snow-locked Rockies, their monetary value was at the centre of a dispute over ownership. Finally, in 1885, the federal government claimed the springs for the people of Canada, establishing the Banff Hot Springs Reserve on land surrounding the springs. It was the beginning of Canada's national park system.

"These springs will recuperate the patient and recoup the treasury," declared Prime Minister John A. Macdonald. He was right: travellers from around the world paid ten cents a swim to bathe in the springs, prompting construction of a complex that housed both the springs and the largest swimming pool on Earth. It remained in use from 1914 until 1976. Nine years later a new hot springs complex was opened, attracting over a million visitors each year.

Elsewhere in the Rockies, hot springs are protected within national parks. People have been soaking in Radium Hot Springs, at the western entrance to Kootenay National Park, since 1911. Now about 350,000 tourists a year come to Radium. Farther north in Jasper National Park, Miette Hot Springs were developed for tourism in 1913.

Opposite: *Banff Hot Springs today.*

Above: Squeezed between the peaks of the Fairholme Range northeast of Banff, Lake Minnewanka's nineteen-kilometre shoreline is accessible by hiking trails. Hikers and tour-boat travellers enjoy views of Mount Inglismaldie's 2,964-metre summit. The largest lake in Banff National Park, Minnewanka's outlet, at the west end, is dammed to provide power for Banff.

Opposite: Johnston Canyon is a favourite spot for birders who come to see black swifts nesting in rock crevices here. The fifteen-metre falls, reached by a twenty-minute hike from Highway 1A, are a popular detour for motorists heading toward Castle Mountain.

Above: A Rocky Mountain bighorn ram stands sentinel from a mountaintop post. Weighing up to 155 kilograms, these wild sheep are prey for wolves and cougars. They are often seen grazing in a meadow on Mount Norquay, above downtown Banff.

Opposite: Above the Bow River valley, the stark, eroded columns of Castle Mountain, shaped by ancient glaciers, are a famous landmark northwest of Banff, near the junction of Highways 1 and 93. Discovered by members of the Palliser Expedition in 1858, the sheer limestone and quartzite faces have become a challenge to modern-day rock climbers.

Lake Louise

It is little wonder Lake Louise is the most famous mountain lake in the world: it is the epitome of postcard perfect. Only 2.4 kilometres long, its emerald waters lie at an elevation of 1,713 metres. Its headwaters funnel down a V-shaped valley, dominated by the glacier-capped summit of Mount Victoria. At 3,464 metres, Mount Victoria stands above its neighbours—Mounts Lefroy and Whyte, The Beehive, and Mount Niblock.

Before the late 1800s this Rocky Mountain jewel was known only to Stoney Indians. Then, in 1882, Tom Wilson, a Canadian Pacific Railway worker, heard what sounded like thunder in the distance while sharing a campsite with local natives. The Indians said it came from a mountain above "the lake of the little fishes." They guided him there and he climbed above the lake to see avalanches thundering down from Victoria Glacier. Wilson called his discovery Emerald Lake, a name later changed to honour Princess Louise Caroline Alberta, fourth daughter of Queen Victoria and wife of Canada's governor-general, the Marquis of Lorne.

The icy waters of Lake Louise are held back by a dam of glacial moraine at its outlet. Below the natural dam, Louise Creek runs down to meet the Bow River, where the community of Lake Louise is home to about eight hundred people. This little village, known as Laggan in 1884, was a base camp for twelve thousand CPR workers when the railway was being pushed over the Continental Divide into British Columbia through Kicking Horse Pass.

Having the means to bring the tourists to the scenery, the CPR's habit was to build accommodation for its passengers.

The first Chateau Lake Louise, built in 1890, was a modest chalet-style building with access from the railway to the lake by crude trail. It burned down two years later and was replaced in 1893 by a larger lodge with road access.

Like Banff, Lake Louise quickly became a gathering place for those who could afford such luxuries. Among them was American climber Philip S. Abbot, of the Boston-based Appalachian Mountain Club. Abbot's failed attempts to scale the 3,423-metre peak of Mount Lefroy in 1895 prompted him to return the following year for a second assault. It was an ill-fated mission, for he died after falling from a steep wall. It was the first climbing fatality in North America.

Rather than discourage would-be challengers, news of Abbot's death lured even more mountaineers to the shores of Lake Louise. A larger, Tudor-style hotel was built in 1899 to accommodate the influx. By 1913 a new wing dwarfed the existing chateau. Shortly after, Lake Louise was linked by road to Banff. When the new hotel wing burned down in 1924, it was replaced in a style that matched the rest of the building. The Chateau Lake Louise was given a new facade in 1984 and yet another wing was added in 1987.

Today the chateau and Lake Louise complement one another. As always, it is a luxurious base for modern-day explorers who come to hike the shoreline trail or climb the valley at the far end of the lake. Energetic hikers and cross-country skiers travel trails to the south, discovering the scenic attributes of Moraine and Eiffel lakes, Wenkchemna Pass, and the Valley of Ten Peaks.

Opposite: *An alpenhorn, like those played by Swiss herders, echoes across the placid waters of Lake Louise. Around the turn of the century, Swiss and Austrian guides often led mountaineering parties to the peaks surrounding Lake Louise.*

Chateau Lake Louise

Unlike other hotels in the Canadian Pacific Railway chain, the Chateau Lake Louise had a humble beginning. Originally a rustic log cabin built on the lakeshore in 1890, it was reached by foot or packhorse from Laggan, a nearby railway camp on the Bow River. After the cabin burned down in 1893, a new building was erected with a second storey. But the hotel could accommodate only a dozen guests and staff were compelled to sleep in tents.

With demand increasing, a new Tudor-style chalet was designed by Francis Rattenbury, the CPR's house architect who drew the plans for many of the railway's hotels. Rattenbury's hotel was expanded in 1912 through the addition of a 350-room concrete complex. Five years later a power plant below the lake brought electricity and all its comforts to the hotel, which now spread along the lakeshore.

With the hotel able to house a thousand guests, the old horse-and-buggy service from Laggan was replaced by a narrow-gauge tramline to shuttle 180 passengers at a time. By 1930, automobiles had become the major mode of transport to Lake Louise.

A few years after the huge Tudor wing burned down in 1924, Rattenbury returned to his homeland, England, where he met his death in 1935 at the hands of his wife's lover.

Opposite: *The Chateau Lake Louise today.*

Above and opposite: *Lake Louise as seen from the chateau at its eastern end is perhaps the world's most famous view of a mountain lake. Fed by meltwater from Victoria Glacier, the frigid emerald lake is dominated by the 3,464-metre summit of Mount Victoria. Though slightly lower, the other peaks above Lake Louise—Mounts Lefroy and Whyte, The Beehive, and Mount Niblock—are no less impressive.*

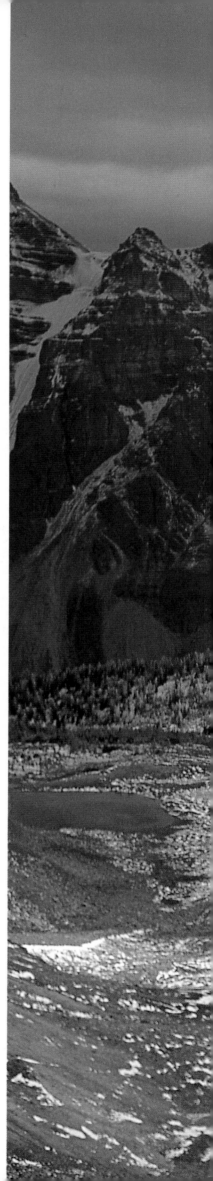

Above: *A hiker stops to absorb the scenery of Larch Valley, south of Lake Louise. A walk through the subalpine larch woods and tundra ponds from Moraine Lake provides excellent views of the Wenkchemna Peaks, west of Larch Valley.*

Opposite: *The Wenkchemna Peaks, on the Continental Divide southwest of Lake Louise, are familiar to Canadians as the image on a twenty-dollar bill. Wenkchemna means ten in the tongue of the Stoney Indians, and this area is often called the Valley of Ten Peaks. These peaks—all in the three-thousand-metre range—span ten kilometres along the skyline above Moraine Lake.*

Swiss Guides

Swiss guide Edward Feuz, Jr. leads a client up Saddleback Mountain, near Lake Louise, in 1910. The Canadian Pacific Railway completed negotiations in 1888 to bring Christian Hasler and Edward Feuz, Sr., the first of many Swiss guides, to Canada.

This was a period when mountaineering in the Rockies was in its heyday, with the challenge of many "first ascents" beckoning those who could afford the train fares, luxury accommodation, and guiding services. The intrepid Swiss, many from Interlaken, completed thousands of climbs, leading many "firsts" in the Rockies. Edward Feuz, Jr. worked in this country for more than forty years, taking clients on seventy-eight "first ascents."

The Alpine Club of Canada's camp in Paradise Valley was a gathering place for European guides. During one visit, a woman named Ethel Jones, like other climbers, was deeply impressed by the guides.

"While we were waiting one of my long cherished dreams came true," she wrote. "I saw a Swiss guide in the flesh. . . . He wore the official badge on his coat lapel. He even sported the Tyrolean feather. His boots were as thick and as full of nails as I had hoped. He carried an ice-axe, a rucksack, and a coiled rope. . . . He was a most satisfying person."

Opposite: Mount Temple, as seen from Saddleback Mountain.

Above: A vigilant pika issues its piercing alarm signal. These hamster-sized rock rabbits build miniature haystacks of dried vegetation to eat through winter, when they hide beneath the snow. They jealously guard their haystacks, warding off would-be thieves by boxing with forepaws or kicking with their hind feet.

Opposite: The 3,542-metre peak of Mount Temple towers over the rushing waters of Moraine Creek. In 1894, at the start of the golden age of mountaineering, this challenging summit was the first to be conquered. Nearly all of the major peaks in the Canadian Rockies were climbed during this era. The last was Mount Robson in 1913.

Above: The Tower of Babel stands apart from other summits above Moraine Lake. The natural dam blocking the lake's outlet is believed to have formed from boulders that tumbled from the tower. The steep quartzite walls of the Tower of Babel are frequently scaled by rock climbers.

Previous pages: The Wenkchemna Peaks reflect from the mirrorlike surface of Moraine Lake, ten kilometres south of Lake Louise. This lovely lake, which rivals Lake Louise for natural beauty, was discovered in 1894, the same year nearby Mount Temple was climbed for the first time. A hiking trail follows the lake's northwest shore.

Fed by meltwater from Wenkchemna Glacier, Moraine Lake's outlet is blocked by boulders of quartzite. This rock, called the Gog Formation, was formed about 550 million years ago on the bottom of an inland sea. Ripple rock, which looks like intertidal sand on a beach, is found near the outlet.

Above and opposite: Grizzlies and black bears inhabit the Rocky Mountain parks, wandering from spawning streams in the valley bottoms to the meadows of the high alpine. A grizzly sow with a cub, as shown here, is particularly dangerous to human intruders. Newborn bear cubs emerge from their dens as winter snows begin to melt. Black bears are seen more frequently in the Rockies than their larger kin.

The Icefields
Parkway

The Icefields Parkway is a 230-kilometre tour through the heartland of the Canadian Rockies. Said to be the most scenic drive in North America, this route captures the essence of the Rocky Mountains—ice-clear rivers and glaciated lakes, roadside elk and black bears, snow-crowned peaks and endless fields of glistening ice.

Completed in 1940, this road was built specifically to display the scenery between Lake Louise and Jasper. It follows the interior valleys along the east side of the Continental Divide. Where the long, narrow finger of Athabasca Glacier reaches down to the road, drivers can step from their vehicles and hear the glacier groan and hiss as meltwater pours into Sunwapta Lake. The glacier drops tonnes of powdered rock into the tiny tarn, giving the lake a muddy hue.

Athabasca Glacier, just within the Jasper National Park boundary, is one of over two dozen glaciers forming the massive Columbia Icefield. A total of 325 square kilometres, its depths range from 100 to 325 metres. This expansive sheet of ice and snow covers a high plateau between Mount Columbia, at 3,737 metres, and Mount Athabasca, at 3,491 metres. It is the largest icefield in the Rocky Mountains and the largest in the continent's subarctic interior.

Straddling the Continental Divide, this huge icefield is known as the "Mother of Rivers." It is the source of waterways that run across North America to three oceans. From the 3,520-metre Snow Dome flow the headwaters of the Athabasca, North Saskatchewan, Fraser, and Columbia river systems.

The Columbia Icefield also affects Rocky Mountain weather. Warm Pacific winds cool as they blow across the icefield, making adjacent valleys colder than others in the Rockies.

This is one of the few places in the world where tourists can explore an icefield by motorized vehicle. During World War I, the military experimented with ice travel, using jeeps, trucks, and snowmobiles. They succeeded in reaching the peak of Snow Dome and actually landed a plane on the icefield. The first "snowcoach," an old bus with a half-track attached to its wheels, ventured onto the ice in 1948. Snowcoach tours on Columbia Icefield today have become one of the most popular attractions in the Rockies: up to three thousand passengers a day take forty-five-minute tours of the ice.

While a quarter-million tourists travel the Columbia Icefield each year, few explore the extensive passageways of Castleguard Cave. Entrances to these dusky grottos appear in meadows near the icefield. Discovered in 1924, the most thorough exploration was carried out in 1980 when a team spent ten days underground, charting eighteen kilometres of corridors. Many of the underground routes, like other places in the Rocky Mountains, remain unexplored.

Opposite: *Since 1940 motorists have enjoyed the most beautiful drive in North America. The Icefields Parkway is a 230-kilometre tour through the heart of the Canadian Rockies from Lake Louise to Jasper. It is one of the few places where travellers can drive to the toe of a glacier.*

Bow Lake/Jimmy Simpson

A teepee is set up on the shores of Bow Lake to accommodate a 1924 expedition to Columbia Icefield. This had been a favourite campsite of the legendary guide, Jimmy Simpson, since he first saw Bow Lake in 1895 with his friend, Bill Peyto. Like Peyto, Simpson began a guiding career in the late 1890s as a camp cook for out-fitter Tom Wilson.

By the turn of the century, Simpson's con-nections had plunged him into a busy career, guiding in summer, hunting and trapping in the lonely outback between Bow Lake and Alex-andra River during winter. He was particularly swift on snowshoes and was nicknamed Nashan-esen by the Stoney Indians, meaning ``wolver-ine-go-quickly.''

Using the stunted trees from the shores of Bow Lake, in 1922 he completed an octagonal lodge there, taking advantage of the short tim-bers. Windows and doors were packed by horse from Laggan, near Lake Louise. As the Banff-Jasper Highway was nearing completion in the late 1930s, Simpson built a new lodge at Bow Lake in 1937, one of only two along the route.

Simpson's son took over his business in the 1940s, but Jimmy Simpson continued to enter-tain guests until his death, at age ninety-five, in 1972. Above Bow Lake, the 3,012-metre summit of Mount Jimmy Simpson looks north to Peyto Lake, both named in honour of two old Rocky Mountain friends.

Opposite: *Bow Lake on the Icefields Parkway.*

Above: Fed by Bow Glacier on the Wapta Icefield, the turquoise-blue waters of Bow Lake greet motorists on the Icefields Parkway. About thirty-six kilometres north of Lake Louise, the lake is the site of Num-ti-jah Lodge, built on the north shore in 1922.

Opposite: Views of the Crowfoot Glacier, named for its odd shape, are seen across Bow Lake from the Icefields Parkway. A roadside viewpoint looking toward the glacier has an interpretive display near the heads of trails leading to Dolomite Pass. This area is the only part of Banff National Park inhabited by woodland caribou.

Bill Peyto

With his broad-brimmed hat, bushy moustache and penetrating blue eyes, outfitter Bill Peyto was the perfect image of a nineteenth-century mountain man. An Englishman, he arrived in Canada at the age of eighteen and became a proficient prospector in the hills around Banff.

His intimate knowledge of the Rockies led him to a career as an outfitter, working for an established guide in the early 1890s. After serving in the Boer War he returned to Canada to become one of the most respected guides in the Rockies. He travelled with many expeditions into the mountain outback, including the 1897 journey that resulted in the discovery of the Columbia Icefield.

The view of the lake below Bow Summit, on the Icefields Parkway, was one of Peyto's favourites and it is appropriate that the lake was named in his honour. It is said the colour of his beloved lake matched his eyes. A nearby peak and one of the glaciers flowing from the Wapta Icefield are also named for "Wild" Bill Peyto.

Like other guides, Peyto took many visitors into the Rocky Mountain wilderness. At season's end, it was guides like Peyto who ensured the backwoods routes they travelled remained cleared for the next year's throng of tourists.

Opposite: *Peyto Lake from a viewpoint near the Icefields Parkway.*

Above: Just inside the southern boundary of Jasper National Park, Wilcox Pass lies along the eastern side of the Icefields Parkway. Discovered in 1896, the pass was easier going than the Sunwapta River valley for horseback explorers travelling the route that later became the Icefields Parkway.

Opposite: About sixty kilometres north of Lake Louise, Waterfowl Lakes, with nesting mallards and goldeneyes, are a widening of the Mistaya River. In the background Mount Chephren, at 3,307 metres, stands to the west of the lakes. This is a popular camping and canoeing spot along the Icefields Parkway.

Columbia Icefield

Rocky Mountain travellers peer into an ice cave at the terminus of Athabasca Glacier in 1914. Athabasca is one of two dozen glaciers comprising the Columbia Icefield, on the border between Banff and Jasper parks. At 325 square kilometres it is the largest icefield in the Rockies and the birthplace of rivers that flow to Canada's three oceans.

Early horse riders avoided the icefields until 1923 when trail guide Jimmy Simpson ventured onto Saskatchewan Glacier with a team of pack horses. His shortcut between Sunwapta Pass, northeast of the Columbia Icefield, and Castleguard Meadows, on the southern side, became a popular journey, known as the Glacier Trail, for people riding between Lake Louise and Jasper.

Twenty-five years later, modern-day adventurers began touring the Columbia Icefield in the first "snowcoach," an old bus modified for travel on the slippery ice. Now a quarter-million people a year take the snowcoach onto Athabasca Glacier.

Although trail rides are still available in the Rocky Mountain parks, most tourists view the icefields from the comfort of their cars by driving the Icefields Parkway. Columbia is the most accessible, but other icefields in the Canadian Rockies include Wapituk, Wapta, Freshfield, Campbell, Mons, Lyell, and Wilson.

Opposite: *The Columbia Icefield Chalet stands at the edge of the icefield.*

Above and opposite: Snowcoach tours, one of the most popular activities in the Rockies, began in 1948 on the Columbia Icefield, the largest in the Canadian Rockies. Now about 250,000 people take the forty-five-minute journey every year.

Overleaf: Beauty Creek, in Sunwapta Valley, is a typical "braided stream." These meandering gravel waterways have multiple channels that fill with meltwater from glaciers and change courses as water levels rise and fall. Beauty Creek, about forty-five kilometres south of Jasper, carries water and silt from the Columbia Icefield.

Jasper
National Park

At 10,800 square kilometres, Jasper National Park is not only the largest in the Canadian Rockies, it is the most mountainous. Less than one-tenth of the park is valley bottoms: most of the landscape is rocks, glaciers, mountain slopes, and alpine meadows.

Some of its peaks rank among the highest in the Canadian Rockies—Mount King Edward at 3,475 metres, Mount Brazeau at 3,470 metres, Stutfield Peak at 3,450 metres, and the conspicuous Mount Edith Cavell at 3,363 metres. Just outside the park boundary, seventy-five kilometres northwest of Jasper townsite, the impressive peak of Mount Robson, known as "The Monarch" by early mountaineers, towers above all others around it. At 3,954 metres, it is the highest in the Canadian Rockies.

Jasper is a land of extremes. Far below these peaks along the Continental Divide, the round and rolling Foothills Ranges occupy a small section of the park. They are the only representation of this type of terrain in the four Rocky Mountain national parks.

Jasper National Park is also the nucleus of one of the truly pristine wilderness regions of the Rocky Mountains. It is adjoined on the north by Alberta's Willmore Wilderness Park, totalling 4,597 square kilometres. B.C.'s Mount Robson Provincial Park, to the northwest, encompasses 2,198 square kilometres; and the 245-square-kilometre Hamber Provincial Park lies to the southwest in B.C.

Together these protected environs are a haven for elk, mule deer, bighorn sheep, and their predatory foes. Many of these wild creatures appear at pastures and roadsides in early morning and evening, giving Jasper a well-deserved reputation as one of the continent's prime viewing areas for big wildlife. Black bears are a frequent sight, but grizzlies, cougars, and timber wolves avoid the company of humans. Most of the 280 bird species found in the Rockies inhabit Jasper National Park.

A thousand kilometres of hiking trails lead outback wanderers into the far reaches of the park. In the north there are paths along the valleys of the Snake Indian, Blue, Smokey, and Deer rivers; in the south you can hike to Poboktan Pass or along Endless Chain Ridge toward Maligne Lake, the largest within the Rocky Mountain parks.

For more sedentary vacationers, many of Jasper's features are accessible by road—Athabasca Glacier, Miette Hot Springs, Sunwapta and Athabasca falls, Mount Edith Cavell, and Maligne Lake. A tramway runs above the treeline to the top of The Whistlers for dramatic views of surrounding peaks and the lakes of the broad Athabasca Valley in the east.

Like other Rocky Mountain parks, Jasper was the offspring of the railroad boom. Anticipating the Great Northern Railway running through Yellowhead Pass, twenty-five kilometres west of Jasper townsite, in 1907 the federal government set aside parkland in the upper Athabasca basin. The Canadian National Railway arrived later, opening Jasper Park Lodge in 1922. Highway 16 follows the railway tracks up the Athabasca Valley to Jasper, then continues over the Continental Divide and into B.C. through Yellowhead Pass. It remains the only east-west route through the park for Jasper's forty-five hundred residents.

Opposite: *All of the water in the Maligne River squeezes through a metre-wide gorge near its confluence with the Athabasca River. Several waterfalls and footbridges are located along Maligne Canyon's two-kilometre length. Silty glacier water continues to scrape about half a centimetre of limestone from the canyon walls each year.*

Above: Angel Glacier points like an icy finger down the north face of Mount Edith Cavell, about twenty kilometres south of Jasper. Hikers in the subalpine forest and alpine meadows here can walk an interpretive loop on the Path of the Glacier trail.

Previous pages: Wapiti, or Rocky Mountain elk, often gather in large herds alongside highways through the Rocky Mountains. Canada's most vocal deer, the high-pitched whistles of these 360-kilogram buglers may be heard across the valleys of the Rockies just before sunset. For mountain travellers, they are among the most visible large animals.

Morning sun reflects from the 3,363-metre summit of Mount Edith Cavell, one of the most noticeable mountains in Jasper National Park. It was named in 1916 for a British nurse who was executed by Germans for helping Allied prisoners of war escape from fallen Brussels.

Above: The tranquil, jade-coloured waters of the Valley of the Five Lakes are a haven for waterfowl, deer, elk, beavers, and other animals. With a network of trails and boardwalks, the woods and marshes here are hiking grounds for birders and wildlife watchers. From some points there are distant views of Mount Edith Cavell's prominent peak.

Opposite: Thirty-two kilometres south of Jasper on the Icefields Parkway, Athabasca Falls are among the most famous in Jasper Park. The falls are particularly attractive during spring freshet as they plunge twelve metres through a narrow quartzite canyon.

Jasper Park Lodge/ Lac Beauvert

Touted as the largest log building in the world, Jasper Park Lodge was built by the Canadian National Railway in 1922 to rival the luxurious hotels of the Canadian Pacific Railway. That same year the first car from Edmonton arrived in Jasper, using the railway bed as a road. Twenty-nine years passed before Highway 16, an all-weather road, joined Edmonton and Jasper.

On the shores of Lac Beauvert beneath the 2,460-metre summit of Roche Bonhomme, the lodge replaced a tent city that had sprung up in 1915. This 1925 photograph was among the last taken at the original lodge: as Jasper's popularity grew, the lodge was expanded in 1927 to accommodate 425 guests. It burned down in 1952 and was replaced, at a cost of 3 million dollars, by the existing lodge.

Jasper House was an important supply post for fur traders during the early 1800s, who travelled up the Athabasca and Whirlpool rivers and over the Continental Divide at Athabasca Pass, about fifty-six kilometres south of Jasper. This remained the main route for fur brigades until the mid-1920s when the North West and Hudson's Bay companies merged. Jasper House was moved farther upstream on the Athabasca River and Yellowhead Pass, twenty-five kilometres west of present-day Jasper, became a new trade route. Highway 16 today is known in B.C. as the Yellowhead Highway.

Opposite: *Jasper Park Lodge, on the shore of Lac Beauvert, sits below the summit of Roche Bonhomme.*

Above: The jaylike Clark's nutcracker breeds at high elevations in the Rockies while deep snow is still on the ground. Carrying nearly a hundred conifer seeds in a sublingual pouch, it may stash thirty thousand seeds and remember the location of a thousand caches.

Previous pages: Pyramid Lake, eight kilometres west of Jasper, is the only lake in Jasper National Park where power boating is allowed. A scenic backdrop to the lake is provided by Pyramid Mountain, rising in the north to 2,766 metres.

Adult hoary marmots, weighing up to six kilograms, are the largest members of the squirrel family. Known as whistlers, their shrill alarms warn other mountain dwellers of impending danger. They live in colonies in the alpine areas of the Rockies, burrowing under boulders to hide from grizzlies and other predators.

Chief Sampson Beaver/
Mary Shaffer

The Rocky Mountains were the homeland of Stoney Chief Sampson Beaver and his family. Chief Beaver provided a crude map for Mary Shaffer, a Quaker widow from Philadelphia, who used the map in 1908 to find Maligne Lake. At twenty-two kilometres long, this largest—and extraordinarily scenic—lake in the Canadian Rockies now is a favourite of tour-boat travellers.

Shaffer had originally arrived in the Rockies as Mary Sharples, a friend of Mary Vaux, whose family was among the early tourists here. Sharples met and married Dr. Charles Shaffer, who was collecting and cataloguing plant specimens. During their annual pilgrimages, Mary Shaffer kept a journal, took photographs and painted the wildflowers they collected.

After the death of her husband in 1903, Shaffer continued her Rocky Mountain sojourns and published an illustrated book, *Old Indian Trails of the Canadian Rockies*, in 1911. The story of her adventures was a success that raised the profile of both Mary Shaffer and the mountains she loved. The book, which describes the region's incomparable beauty and its value as an area for study and wilderness pleasures, was recently reprinted as A *Hunter of Peace*.

At the age of fifty, Mary Shaffer turned to a more sedentary life, retiring in Banff until her death in 1939.

Opposite: *Maligne Lake and Spirit Island.*

Above and opposite: A total of 4,597 square kilometres, Willmore Wilderness Park was created in 1959 as Alberta's largest provincial park. Only a few rough roads invade this immense outback north of Jasper National Park. Beyond Willmore, the Rockies leave Alberta and continue for another eight hundred kilometres through northern British Columbia to the Liard Plateau, on the Yukon border.

Previous pages: Twenty-two kilometres long, Maligne is the largest lake in the Canadian Rockies. Tour boats ply its emerald waters, running the shorelines below the 3,525-metre peak of Mount Brazeau. Hikers can walk to Shaffer Viewpoint above the lake for spectacular views of Leah and Samson peaks and Mounts Unwin and Charlton.

Mount Robson

Members of the Alpine Club of Canada, who were largely responsible for introducing the public to the Rocky Mountain outback, peer into the icy depths of Robson Glacier on an expedition in 1913. This was the first year that mountaineers successfully climbed high above the glacier to the 3,954-metre summit of Mount Robson, the highest in the Canadian Rockies.

Before 1913 there had been five failed bids to reach Robson's peak. Each foiled attempt seemed to taunt members of the Alpine Club, whose president insisted the first ascent be made by a Canadian. It was arranged for Conrad Kain, an Austrian-born mountain guide, to lead two men to the top.

''I expect to have hard and possibly dangerous work,'' Kain wrote before the ascent. ''Mount Robson is a wicked peak.'' Despite his warnings, two men, Bill Foster, deputy minister of public works for B.C., and Albert ''Mack'' MacCarthy, an American from Summit, New Jersey, accepted the challenge.

Plagued by intense cold and blowing snow, they launched an assault on the northeast face of the mountain, inching their way up a series of steep fifteen- and twenty-metre ice walls. Just a few footsteps from the summit, Kain turned to his clients and announced with a smile: ''Gentlemen, that's as far as I can take you.''

Opposite: *Mount Robson, the highest peak in the Canadian Rockies.*

Yoho
National Park

In the language of the Cree people, "Yoho" expresses awe. It is a fitting honorific for this 1,313-square-kilometre tract of mountains, meadows, and forests. Yoho National Park's highest point, Mount Goodsir at 3,562 metres, is one of twenty-eight peaks over 3,000 metres within the park. There are at least twenty-five glacial lakes here—Oesa, McArthur, Morning Glory, Opabin, Wapta, and more. Flowing in and around the lakes are countless streams that feed rivers such as the Kicking Horse, Yoho, and Amiskwi. Along the waterways are the waterfalls for which Yoho is best known—Takakkaw, Twin, Laughing, and Wapta.

The powerful erosive forces of glaciers, wind, and running water are conspicuously displayed throughout the park. Torrents of water have worn a hole through a solid rock bed, creating a natural rock bridge over the Kicking Horse River. Hoodoos—spires of glacial silt, often precariously crowned by teetering boulders—stand like sentinels. Formed in the wake of moving glaciers, they have been whipped by wind and bombarded by rain and snow.

Entirely on the British Columbia side of the Continental Divide, Yoho National Park, unlike Banff or Jasper, is often enveloped by masses of moist, warm Pacific air. As these weather fronts collide with the divide, the moisture descends onto Yoho, nourishing forests resembling those of Canada's west coast: western red cedar, devil's club, western hemlock, and other coastal species grow in wetbelt pockets throughout the park.

Another feature that distinguishes Yoho from neighbouring parks is the Burgess Shale site, one of the world's most fascinating fossil beds. On the slopes of Mount Stephen, overlooking the town of Field, this unusual collection of preserved organisms was discovered in the 1870s by a railway surveyor. But the scientific community didn't get wind of it until 1909 when a paleontologist from the Smithsonian Institution chanced upon the fossils during a geological expedition.

More than 140 species of marine invertebrates—sponges, sea worms, and other buglike creatures—lay intact between layers of hardened sediment. Some of these animals lived here 530 million years ago. In 1981, more than a century after their discovery, the Burgess Shale fossil beds were declared a UNESCO World Heritage Site.

More than four hundred kilometres of trails reach the highlights of Yoho. Among the many walks is a thirteen-kilometre trek to Lake O'Hara. Not surprisingly, this jade-coloured gem is strikingly similar to Banff National Park's famous Lake Louise. Two peaks that dominate the view from Lake Louise—Mounts Victoria and Lefroy—also loom above Lake O'Hara, but from the opposite side of the Continental Divide.

For years Takakkaw Falls, a precipitous drop on the Yoho River, enjoyed a reputation as Canada's highest waterfalls: the height, by some references, was claimed to be 503 metres, rivalling Vancouver Island's 440-metre Della Falls, the nation's next-highest. In 1985, however, surveyors from the Canadian Parks Service recalculated Takakkaw's height at 254 metres. Despite this diminishment, the falls have retained their awe-inspiring prominence.

Yoho began as a small reserve along the Canadian Pacific Railway line near Mount Stephen in 1886. The smallest of Canada's adjoining Rocky Mountain national parks, it is a natural example of how good things come in small packages.

Opposite: *The azure waters of Lake McArthur sparkle beneath Mount Biddle on the eastern edge of Yoho National Park. Near the Continental Divide on the western slopes of the Bow Range, this lake receives few visitors compared to neighbouring Lake O'Hara. Lake McArthur is reached by hiking trail.*

Above: Mountain goats high on the rocky slopes often look like distant, off-white boulders to passing motorists. Despite skidproof soles on their hooves, mountain goats occasionally slip from the cliffs to their deaths, providing fresh carrion for ravens, eagles, coyotes, and other scavengers.

Opposite: Lake O'Hara, touted by some as the most scenic in the Canadian Rockies, lies behind the more famous Lake Louise, on the opposite side of the Continental Divide. Lake O'Hara and its lodge can be reached by a thirteen-kilometre shuttle bus, but many prefer to take in the scenery at a hiker's pace.

Above: The 2,583-metre peak of Mount Burgess rises above Emerald Lake, near the centre of Yoho. Covering 116 hectares, the lake is the park's largest. Renovations at Emerald Lake Lodge, built by the Canadian Pacific Railway in 1902, were completed in 1986.

Opposite: Wiwaxy Peaks are among the many outback destinations in Yoho National Park. Reached by trails near Lake O'Hara, the weather-worn Wiwaxy Lodge offered welcome shelter for hikers exploring alpine meadows here in the early part of this century.

Above: Takakkaw Falls, a precipitous 254-metre drop in the Yoho River, are perhaps the best-known landmark in Yoho National Park. Daly Glacier fuels the falls with meltwater that joins the Yoho River just upstream of the falls. Dauntless ice climbers scale the frozen cascade in winter.

Opposite: The Kicking Horse River's Natural Bridge is an example of the powerful natural force of rushing water. The river has pounded a hole beneath the limestone that once dammed the river. This unusual feature is located near the confluence of the Kicking Horse, Emerald, and Amiskwi rivers.

Canadian Pacific Railway/ Kicking Horse River

The Canadian Pacific Railway follows the Kicking Horse River in Yoho National Park. Undeniably the greatest engineering accomplishment of the day, the CPR's crossing of the Rocky Mountains taxed the talents of its builders to the limit.

The brainchild of Prime Minister John A. Macdonald, the transcontinental railway was designed to lure the western colony of British Columbia into Canadian Confederation. Although B.C. became a province in 1871, it wasn't until 1885 that "a plain iron spike welded East to West" at Craigellachie, B.C.

During nearly five years of construction, thirty thousand workers laid the tracks. As they moved west from the Prairies, they followed the Bow River through Banff and northwest to Lake Louise. The route then turned west through Kicking Horse Pass over the Continental Divide. The steep grades from the pass down to the Rocky Mountain Trench presented a formidable challenge: speeding trains were often forced to veer off into runaway lanes. Finally, in 1909, the grade was softened by the Spiral Tunnels, train-sized corkscrew-shaped shafts blasted through the western side of Kicking Horse Pass.

Construction of the railway and its luxurious hotels was the impetus behind creation of the country's national parks system. Banff National Park, the first in Canada, was designated the same year, and the same month, that the CPR was completed.

Opposite: *British Columbia's Kicking Horse River.*

Kootenay
National Park

Unlike its neighbouring parks, Kootenay National Park has no roots in railways. It was the product of a failed road-building project that was rescued by the Canadian government.

Windermere Lake, in the Rocky Mountain Trench to the west, showed potential as an agricultural region, but there was no road to eastern markets. So in 1910 the B.C. government began construction of a highway to Banff, but soon ran out of money. The project lay dormant until after World War I when B.C. offered land for a national park on both sides of the highway. In return, the federal government completed the road and designated the park in 1920.

The road, Highway 93, remains a long and leisurely scenic route through the Kootenay and Vermilion river valleys of southeastern British Columbia. It is the only transportation corridor through this 1,406-square-kilometre mountain wilderness, leaving much of Kootenay National Park to the wildlife. Though more than two hundred kilometres of hiking trails crisscross the park, many areas rarely see a human visitor.

Kootenay is perhaps best known for its bubbling hot mineral pools at Radium Hot Springs, near the western gateway to the park. The steaming springs emerge from the Earth at a temperature of forty-three degrees Celsius. They are diverted to an aquacourt where bathers warm their bones in the crisp mountain air. Early natives soaked in these clear, odourless springs for medicinal purposes; many modern-day travellers make annual pilgrimages to Radium to ease the pains of rheumatism or arthritis. In all, about 350,000 people a year visit Radium Hot Springs.

Visitors who enter the park through the west entrance pass the portals of Sinclair Canyon, where the highway winds through a narrow gorge and runs up to Sinclair Pass. From here there are stunning views down the broad, lush valley of the Kootenay River, wedged between the Vermilion and Brisco ranges.

At the opposite end of the Banff-Windermere Highway, some cold underground springs seep into the Paint Pots, where red iron oxide, or ochre, is naturally deposited at large pools over an area of about five hundred square metres. Kootenai Indians used the ochre to make vermilion paint and adorn their bodies and homes. Their prehistoric pictographs embellish nearby rocks.

Not far from the Paint Pots, Marble Canyon is a constricted gorge lined by shiny, polished rock. Between three and eighteen metres wide, the canyon at places is up to thirty-nine metres deep. Above the canyon, Vermilion Pass, at an elevation of 1,651 metres, climbs over the Continental Divide, joining Kootenay and Banff national parks.

These mineral pools, high viewpoints, and narrow chasms provide only a portion of Kootenay National Park's scenery. It is known for its hanging glaciers and is the only national park to have both glaciers and cacti. Like other parts of B.C.'s Kootenay region, wildlife here is abundant: while grizzlies, wolves, and cougars are seldom seen, elk, deer, coyotes, bighorn sheep, mountain goats, moose, black bears, and a multitude of birds are fair game for photographers and other wildlife watchers.

Opposite: *McLeod Meadows bring natural colour to the southern section of Kootenay National Park. Overlooking the broad Kootenay River valley, a campground near the meadows is the starting point for a trek to tiny Dog Lake. Summer hikers here may find western wood lilies in bloom.*

Highways / Sinclair Canyon

In 1923 a well-equipped wilderness worshipper motors through Sinclair Canyon, near the western entrance to Kootenay National Park. It was this road, Highway 93 linking Banff to Windermere, B.C., that caused the creation of this park. The B.C. government swapped parkland for the road, which was built by the federal government in the early 1920s.

Railways and horseback guides held a monopoly on transportation in the Rocky Mountain parks until the early 1900s. A few courageous motorists bounced into the parks along railway beds. A road from Calgary reached the gates of Banff National Park in 1909, but it wasn't until after the appointment in 1911 of James B. Harkin, Canada's first commissioner of parks, that automobiles began to tour the parks. Noting a trend toward car travel, Harkin believed the nation's parks should not be the exclusive playgrounds of those who could afford the fares and posh hotels of the railways.

Taking the Canadian Pacific Railway route up the Bow River, the road from Banff was pushed through to Lake Louise, with the help of prison labour, by 1920. From Lake Louise, where the railway turned west, a highway north to Jasper followed the Bow, Mistaya, North Saskatchewan, Sunwapta, and Athabasca rivers. It was completed in 1940. It wasn't until 1962, however, that Highway 1, the Trans-Canada, was officially opened, taking visitors across the Rockies and over the Continental Divide through Yoho National Park's Kicking Horse Pass.

Opposite: *Sinclair Canyon, near the western entrance to Kootenay National Park.*

Above: The cougar, Canada's largest wildcat, may measure three metres from nose to tail and weigh fifty kilograms. It can take an elk or moose three or four times its size. These elusive predators are seldom seen by people in the Rockies. Though they follow the seasonal migrations of their prey, they generally prefer lightly forested, rugged terrain.

Opposite: A tangle of twigs near the top of a Douglas fir in Kootenay National Park is home to a bald eagle and its two offspring. Each spring eagles add new material to their nests, which eventually become so heavy they may topple to the ground. Nests that remain intact might be used repeatedly for half a century.

Overleaf: Rising on the western edge of the Continental Divide, the Vermilion River runs down to the Kootenay River. Influenced by moist air flowing across British Columbia from the Pacific, parts of the forests along the banks of the Vermilion River resemble those of the coast.

Kananaskis
Country

Through the foresight of the people of Alberta, Kananaskis Country was rescued from industrial development in the 1970s. After a series of public forums, they decided this part of the Foothills and Front ranges, southeast of Banff National Park, should be set aside for skiing, hiking, canoeing, fishing, cycling, snowmobiling, birding, and nature conservation.

Preservation of the Kananaskis Valley and surrounding environs has been an on-again-off-again affair since the advent of Banff National Park. It was originally included in the national park, but industrialists successfully lobbied for its exclusion. For decades their ventures enjoyed little control: trees were felled for railway ties, coal was mined in the hills, grasslands were turned to pastures, wildlife was heavily hunted, and hydroelectric dams blocked the streams.

The first dam was built in the early 1900s on the Bow River, east of its confluence with the Kananaskis River. Then, in the early 1930s, a spillway was constructed on Upper Kananaskis Lake, permanently altering the flow of the Kananaskis system. Although the dams remain today, logging and mining are gone.

Captain John Palliser, who explored Kananaskis Country on behalf of the British government in 1858, declared the region beautiful but unfit for white settlers. However, it seemed to suit the Stoney and Sarcee Indians: archaeological digs in this century have unearthed stone tools and other artifacts that suggest Kananaskis Country has been inhabited for eight thousand years.

Today this fifty-two-hundred-square-kilometre protected area is used mainly for conservation and recreation. Within its boundaries are three major provincial parks—Bow Valley in the north, Bragg Creek in the east, and Peter Lougheed park, encompassing Upper and Lower Kananaskis lakes. The region has been divided into various zones and developed for different uses. There are more than a thousand kilometres of hiking trails, a thirty-six-hole golf course, fish ponds, lodges, and accommodation for people who are disabled. The Olympic Nordic Centre, near Canmore, was built in the north end of Kananaskis Country for the 1988 winter Olympics. A unique man-made feature of the area is a network of paved paths for summer cycling and winter ski touring.

Travellers exploring Kananaskis Country find four distinct natural zones that change with elevation. Around the two-thousand-metre level are barren alpine areas of rock, saxifrage, and lichen bordering the glaciers east of the Continental Divide. Farther down are alpine meadows with colourful wildflowers surrounding groves of whitebark pine and larch. Below the alpine, wrens, thrushes, warblers, and other birds find sanctuary in forests of spruce and fir. At the lowest elevations are rolling sandstone foothills with patches of aspen and lodgepole pine growing amid the dry, grassy fields. These lower elevations are home to black bears, moose, coyotes, deer, and a variety of birds and smaller animals.

Kananaskis Country, bounded on the north by the Bow River and on the south by the Highwood River, is bisected by Highway 40, the Kananaskis Highway, which runs through the heart of the recreation area. Highwood Pass, at 2,206 metres, is said to be the highest paved road in Canada.

As the scars of earlier abuses here continue to heal, Kananaskis Country stands as an example of how lands ravaged by past industrialization can be restored.

Opposite: *The snowy slopes of Mount Allan, seven kilometres west of Spray Lakes Reservoir, became a playground for downhill skiers when new facilities, including a lodge, were built for the 1988 Winter Olympics. Ribbon Creek, at the base of the mountain, is known for its rich fossil beds. Snails and clams are among thirty-eight species preserved in the shale and siltstone here.*

Above: The Three Sisters, with the highest peak at 2,970 metres, lie between Canmore, Alberta, and Spray Lakes Reservoir and are visible from the Trans-Canada Highway. The spectacular cliffs of mottled grey limestone are typical of the mountains in this area. Snails, brachiopods, and other fossils of the late Devonian period are locked within these hills.

Opposite: Golfers enjoy views of Mounts Kidd and Chester and other peaks in the three-thousand-metre range that surround the thirty-six-hole Kananaskis Country Golf Course. The course, which lies in the Kananaskis River valley at an elevation of nearly fifteen hundred metres, is known for its white sand traps.

Above: The Z-shaped folds of Mount Kidd are visible from Highway 40, which runs through the heart of Kananaskis Country. This odd geological formation is part of a major fault that runs south to Waterton Lakes National Park. Hikers can follow trails along the Kananaskis River and Ribbon Creek and up Galatea Creek to Lillian Lake.

Opposite: A coyote rests amid the wildflowers of the Kananaskis grasslands. Like the red fox, the coyote is widespread but not abundant in the Canadian Rockies. Feeding on rodents, birds, and insects, a full-grown coyote may weigh thirteen kilograms, about a third as much as a wolf.

Overleaf: The scrubby meadows around Pocaterra Fenn, between Highway 40 and the Kananaskis Lakes, are prime birding territory; mountain bluebirds, black swifts, and a variety of shorebirds are commonly found in the Rockies' Front Ranges. Sparrows-Egg Lake, Pocaterra Creek, and other features of the area are accessible by hiking trails.

Waterton Lakes
National Park

Waterton Lakes National Park is where the mountains meet the Prairies. Peaks to nearly three thousand metres in the Border Ranges of the Rockies bisect the park, shielding the eastern side from moist Pacific air that blows across British Columbia. On the western side of the divide, dense forests of red cedar, hemlock, fir, spruce, larch, and pine blanket the slopes. On the east, the mountains give way to a sea of grasslands stretching across the Canadian Prairies.

These extremes in elevation and climate produce a diversity of flora and fauna. This is prime habitat for bighorn sheep and mountain goats, elk, moose, whitetail and mule deer, grizzly and black bears, wolves, beavers, and other mammals, including a herd of bison maintained by the park. Ptarmigan, eagles, ospreys, trumpeter swans, loons, and a variety of smaller birds are among 250 species listed in the park over the past century.

Waterton lies at a floral crossroads, where plants from the northern and southern mountains meld with species from the Prairies and west coast. Eight hundred flower species are among thirteen hundred types of plants at Waterton. Beargrass, gentian, heather, glacier lilies, and a multitude of other alpine flowers burst into bloom for a few short weeks before autumn snows. Farther down, the grasslands are coloured by pasqueflowers, lupines, Indian paintbrush, asters, shooting stars, and more. Over half of the plant species in Alberta occur in Waterton Lakes National Park, including 125 of the 360 plants considered rare in the province. Thirty-five are deemed nationally rare.

The three Waterton Lakes form the centrepiece of the park. Upper Waterton, at 152 metres, is the deepest lake in the Canadian Rockies and the deepest in Alberta. Although glaciers no longer exist in the park, the streams and lakes are icy cold throughout the year.

Waterton Lakes was once the homeland of the Blackfoot Nation, whose numbers dwindled during the 1800s with the arrival of Europeans. The park has the second-highest density of archaeological sites—more than two hundred—in the Canadian Rockies. The highest is near Crowsnest Pass, just north of the park. Artifacts found here indicate the region was occupied by humans eleven thousand years ago. Today no natives live in the park, but the Blood Indian reserve, north of Waterton Lakes, is inhabited by four thousand people.

Waterton townsite, near the centre of the park, has about a hundred year-round residents. Many of the 650,000 annual visitors travel from Waterton along the Akamina Parkway through the historic Cameron Valley, site of western Canada's first oil well.

Other roads lead over rolling prairie through Blakiston Valley to Red Rock Canyon, providing views of Mount Blakiston, at 2,940 metres the park's highest peak. Hikers travel the backcountry on 183 kilometres of trails.

Declared parkland in 1895, Waterton Lakes is the fourth-oldest and one of the smallest national parks in Canada. Its 525 square kilometres lie entirely within Alberta, snuggled against British Columbia's Akamina-Kishinena Recreation Area. In 1932, Waterton Lakes National Park was united with Montana's Glacier National Park to the south, forming the world's first International Peace Park. In the 1970s these parks were designated as UNESCO Biosphere Reserves, preserving their biological and genetic diversity.

Opposite: *Red Rock Canyon, accessible by a parkway built in 1920, is one of the most colourful landmarks in the Canadian Rockies. Located in the north end of Waterton Lakes National Park, the 1.5-billion-year-old oxidized argillite once sat below ancient tidal mud flats. Hikers who walk the trails around the canyon may see bighorn sheep, which have become accustomed to human visitors.*

Above: Mount Custer's 2,707-metre peak is mirrored in the glass-calm surface of Cameron Lake. The lighter shades of green on this mountain are avalanche paths, where tonnes of tumbling snow cut a swath through the forest. These sunlit openings produce nutritious vegetation for bears, moose, deer, and elk. The cow parsnip here attracts grizzlies.

Opposite: The glacier that carved the cirque filled by the waters of Cameron Lake has vanished from Waterton Lakes National Park, but the moraine deposited by the glacier continues to hold the water in the lake. This lovely waterway, a favourite among canoeists, straddles the Canada-U.S. border and lies within national parks in both countries.

Above: *Mule deer, close relatives of whitetail deer, are abundant in Waterton Lakes National Park where they browse on plants, grasses, and brush at forest edges. Known as jumping deer, they leap over high obstacles and run erratic courses to escape enemies. Mule deer are plentiful on the Prairies and appear to be expanding their range northward.*

Opposite: *Blakiston Creek was once part of the Buffalo Trail, which crossed South Kootenay Pass over the Continental Divide. Today the creek and Blakiston Falls are enjoyed by hikers exploring the northern reaches of Waterton Lakes National Park. The creek, which passes the mouth of Red Rock Canyon, is part of the Waterton River watershed.*

Previous pages: *Opened in 1927, the Prince of Wales Hotel was the last in a chain of luxury hotels built by the Great Northern Railway. The seven-storey structure is the largest wood-frame building in Alberta. The elegant old hotel overlooks Waterton townsite, where Upper and Middle Waterton lakes meet. Early visitors to the hotel travelled into Montana's Glacier National Park aboard the 250-passenger launch International.*

PHOTO CREDITS

Michael E. Burch   pp. 2-3, 3, 11, 14, 20-21, 22-23, 28, 29, 37, 38-39, 52, 55, 61, 62-63, 64-65, 68-69, 73, 76, 90-91, 91, 93, 98-99, 99, 100-101, 102, 103

Halle Flygare   pp. 36-37, 40-41, 46-47, 85

Chris Harris / First Light   p. 72

Bob Herger   pp. 25, 44, 45, 58-59, 80

Thomas Kitchin / First Light   pp. 4-5, 10, 12, 13, 16-17, 24, 26-27, 30, 54, 60, 82-83, 84, 86-87, 92, 94-95

J.A. Kraulis   pp. 74-75

Wayne Lynch   p. 31

Patrick Morrow / First Light   pp. 42-43, 88

Steve Short / First Light   pp. vii, 6-7, 19, 20, 32, 34-35, 48, 50-51, 53, 56-57

John Sylvester / First Light   p. 77

Ron Watts / First Light   pp. viii, 8-9, 70, 96

Darwin Wiggett / First Light   pp. 18, 41, 66, 67, 75, 78-79

All archival photographs are from the Whyte Museum of the Canadian Rockies, Banff, Alberta as follows:

Edward Feuz collection   p. 19
Byron Harmon collection   pp. 5, 6, 43, 69, 79, 83
George Noble collection   p. 63
Royal Ontario Museum   p. 57
Vaux Family collection   p. 17
Mary Schaffer Warren collection   p. 29
Walter D. Wilcox collection   p. 32